PLANTING
SEEDS
of Hope

Christ Unfailing Love

JOYCE LEWIS

ISBN 978-1-964462-93-6 (Paperback)
ISBN 978-1-964462-94-3 (Ebook)

Inquiries and Book Orders should be addressed to:

Leavitt Peak Press
17901 Pioneer Blvd Ste L #298, Artesia, California 90701
Phone #: 2092191548

CONTENTS

INTRODUCTION

*P*lanting Seeds of Hope is the story of Christ's saving grace in my life. After living through many years of painful insecurities and dysfunctional relationships, Christ met me right where I was. He showed me His love and compassion, even before I was a Christian. He sent angels to support me through the trials; His strength kept me going, and His love made it possible for me to find true love. Christ opened doors for me to make critical decisions that were not always in accordance to scripture. Although Christ was leading me to His path and giving me freedom to make my own choices, I realized I needed to get help. The things I experienced were all part of Christ's plan to enable me to understand how I was broken and how much I needed Him.

I have written this book to share my life journey to inspire other women to know his love and believe that He is waiting for them to pursue a relationship with Him.

My happily ever after story began after I met the love of my life, and we began our journey together. We married, started a business together, traveled halfway around the world, and were blessed with a large blended family. We also found time to volunteer and help others. Sure, we had our share of problems, and we sometimes made unwise choices. Christ was always there to get us through.

Placing Christ at the center of our relationship made it possible for us to open our hearts and minds to a new life; one filled with excitement, challenges, adventure, fun, romance, and a passion to grow in our faith.

The foundation of our faith came from the churches we have attended for the last twenty-nine years. We met at Crystal Cathedral in Garden Grove, California, were married there, and remained members there for fourteen years. We then moved to Boulder City, Nevada and became a member of Central Christian Church in Henderson, Nevada for eleven years. At Central, I accepted Jesus as my savior. I was baptized there, became a member, and started a ministry. For the last three years, we have been attending Faith Christian Church in Boulder City, Nevada.

For me, finishing well means communicating with Jesus and following His lead. He will be with me through the transformation from my earthly life to my eternal life. My prayer for everyone is to grow in faith, by building a relationship with Jesus Christ and to truly understand the unconditional love He has for each of us.

DEDICATION

*P*lanting Seeds of Hope is dedicated to Jesus Christ, My Lord and Savior. This book is a gratitude letter for all the blessings He has given me and my husband.

Dearest Jesus,

Thank you for loving me through the painful years in my life. You ever so gently healed me from the many unhealthy emotions I had been living with and gave me the ability to understand how important it is to forgive. When there was doubt Lord, it was you who assured me of your ability to work through the Holy Spirit. You gave me the confidence and the strength to make good choices. As I learned submission, You gave me courage to change my life to reflect Your will and love. I am grateful for the intimate relationship that You and I have. As you revealed my sins through the Holy Spirit, I was able to break the Devil's hold over me. You gave me the wisdom to recognize Satan's evil traps.

You also blessed our finances and gave us great vision. You sent leaders and friends to support and encourage us. Through your teaching, you revealed to me my purpose, and that purpose has become my destiny: You opened the doors of opportunity for me to plant seeds of hope in others.

There are no words to describe my feelings for You. Thank You for continuing to give my husband and I your peace and joy. Finishing well to me is serving You.

With my eternal love,
One of your students

ACKNOWLEDGEMENTS

Without my husband's support and encouragement, I would not be writing this book. God planted seeds of love in his heart, and he has always supported me in my faith and ministry.

Thanks to all our family members who have encouraged me and loved me through the long journey.

Laura, thank you for all the years that you have been there for us. We appreciate your loving kindness; you have been a ray of sunshine in our life.

We have always felt blessed to have friendships that filled our life with joy.

To all our friends and neighbors: Thank you for your caring and kindness. I couldn't get over how some of you seemed to show up when we needed you most.

I would like to thank all the Transitions women for sharing their testimonies and for all their years of faithfulness. I will always treasure the memories of our years together. My prayer is that their testimonies will be a blessing to all women.

To all my PEO sisters: You have been so supportive, generous, and kind to me; thank you from my heart to yours. Thank you Lois, for encouraging me and giving your time to edit parts of my book. I will be forever grateful.

Praise be to the Lord for guiding us to all the churches that gave us scripture-based wisdom and encouragement. My thanks and blessings to all the ministers for their prayers, support, and comments.

PASTORS' COMMENTS

*J*oyce Lewis is the walking embodiment of 2 Corinthians 1:3,4.
God comforts us so we can comfort others with the comfort we
have received. Joyce walked out of a dark situation and discovered
that her life experience perfectly equipped her to assist others in the
journey. Her power comes not only from her own story of redemption
and freedom, but a delightful optimism of spirit that welcomes others
who are seeking to be free from the clutches of emotional abuse. I am
so glad that Joyce has put her story into a book and my prayer is that
her book would be a force of encouragement for others just like Joyce.
Steve Cuss
Lead Pastor
Discovery Church
Broomfield, Colorado

Love never gives up, never looks back and always trusts God.
That statement represents Joyce Lewis. She has been through fire
yet her attitude is that she is too blessed to be depressed. Through
Christ she has become a victor and is no longer a victim. She has
seen God at work in her life and tells that story in this book. Joyce
has become a friend and a support to this church and ministry. I'm
glad that Faith Christian Church has had a little piece in Joyce's
journey. She and her husband Bob have become part of our church
family and demonstrate the love of God in Christ in their everyday
lives. Joyce cares about people and wants to see hurting people find
the loving touch of God who wants us to experience emotional and
spiritual healing. Joyce and Faith Christian Church believe that the

key to life is not the duration but the donation. We live to give. Have you found your purpose in life through Christ? Your life matters. God has a task for you to complete. Don't just count the years but make the years count. The roots of happiness grow deepest in the soil of service. May this book inspire that attitude in you as well.
Pastor Brent Williams
Faith Christian Church,
Boulder City, Nevada

ENDORSEMENT

Pastor Jud Wilhite

I've seen Joyce's servant's heart and faithfulness again and again. She loves God and people, and she seeks to bring encouragement to everyone. And this is exactly what she does in this book. Her story along with the many lives she has intersected with will all point you to the greatest story of all—the story of God's love manifest in Jesus. May this book bring great hope and encouragement to all who read it."

Jud Wilhite, author of Pursued, Sr. Pastor of Central Christian Church

CHAPTER ONE

LIVING WITHOUT FAITH

H ave you ever felt that your life was being lived in a maze? I spent many years wandering from one path to another—lost. Inevitably, each path ended with feelings of disappointment, rejection, and decreased self-worth. God gave me the survival skills that I needed to keep me from any catastrophic life-threating experiences. Before I knew Him, He was watching over me.

In a perfect world, parents are a child's first line of defense while growing up. My father was eighteen and my mother was twenty when they were married, kids themselves. My mother lost both of her parents when she was ten years old and my father was a teenager who grew up in a dysfunctional family. Needless to say, they lacked parenting skills. My sister and I had very little family time with our parents. My father worked at night, my mother worked during the day, and we seldom went to church. Therefore, my chidhood passed in survival mode. It was definitely not what you would call an emotionally healthy family environment.

My high school and young adult years were defined by new experiences and adventures. I lacked clear goals and lived in the moment. I wasn't afraid. At times, I felt lost, but I was never lonely. Years passed before I truly began to understand what it meant to have a true relationship with the Lord and to totally depend on Him for guidance. When you have no clear direction, you keep moving around to find a place to land, to belong. My mother encouraged me to take all the secretarial skill classes that were offered. In the fifties, most of the girls either married or started working in an office after high school. Only the rich girls could afford to go to a four-year college.

Just before graduating, I moved in with my sister and spent the summer at the beach. At summer's end, I started looking for a job. Not many job opportunities existed in Manhattan Beach, California, in those days, so I decided to seek work through a Los Angeles employment agency. I luckily landed a receptionist position with a large medical company. My days were eight hours of working and two hours on the bus (one hour spent each way).

After listening to the wrong people and making decisions based strictly on feelings and emotions, I suffered the pain of learning things the hard way. I felt I had the experience of a twenty-one-year-old, but I was only eighteen.

My sister married, so I moved back in with my parents. I was going through depression after my first love left me. I shared this with my cousin, and she suggested I move to Nebraska and stay with her and her family.

Change was definitely something I thought I needed, and the timing seemed right, so I went to the bus station and bought a ticket to Omaha, Nebraska. I was eighteen and travelling by bus alone halfway across the country. On the way, I met three Air Force young men who were headed to what is now Offutt Air Force Base in Omaha. They were like older brothers looking out for their little sister during our trip together. Sometimes God sends angels to look out for you when you are alone. We got acquainted, played cards, and enjoyed each other's company. Passing the time with the guys made the trip a lot shorter.

The next day, I arrived at my cousin's house in Lincoln, Nebraska, and was greeted by her and her family—her husband and two sons. The house they lived in had a basement with an extra room, which became my room. My cousin was very good to me; it was good to live with family. Another cousin lived close by, and they became like my brothers and sisters.

Once again, working behind the scenes, God opened another door of opportunity. After work one afternoon, my cousin's husband told me about a secretarial position working for a major who was in charge of training commissioned and non-commissioned National Guard officers. My cousin also worked at the armory, so we could ride to work together.

I loved working for the major; he was a great boss. About twenty men and two women worked at the armory, and we always had a good time during our breaks and at lunch. One of the highlights working for the major was that he invited me to go to Camp Ripley in Minnesota where the Guard was training for two weeks. I helped the guys load equipment on to the trucks that were leaving to camp, and they came up with this bright idea that they could get a uniform for me, and I could ride up to camp with them. I went to camp with my female cousin, for the weekend. We were there for the military review. All the different National Guard units and the new commissioned officers would be parading in front of the grandstand where we were sitting with all the VIPs.

After I returned from Minnesota, I started working at the state house for a lieutenant colonel. He asked me to continue working for him, but after working at the Armory with its casual environment, I couldn't see myself working at the state house's formal atmosphere. I gave my notice, got on a train, and went back to California.

Immediately, I started searching for a job after I returned, and I finally found one at Savings & Loan Bank as a teller. After work on Wednesdays, a few of us would head over to a local restaurant and bar for a twenty-five-cent spaghetti dinner. It was there that I met my first husband; his brother introduced us. I didn't pay too much attention to him when he came to the restaurant, though. I was dating someone else at the time. Then, the company I worked for was planning a houseboat trip to Catalina for its employees (I had broken up with the person I was dating), so I decided to ask my ex-husband; he accepted my invitation.

I learned that he had recently returned from Italy, and after being discharged from the Army, he started working part-time and going to school. He was nice, good-looking, and he had a good plan for the future. We were attracted to one other and started dating; the time was right for both of us. We had a lot in common and we believed we could have a future together. Six months after we met, we married.

It was after we married, that we really got to know one another. We had a baby girl the first year of our marriage and two years later, a boy. We both loved our babies and did the best we could to become a family, without either of us having any real family experience ourselves. I stayed home with the babies, and he worked. At the time, this is what we both wanted. We moved into to a brand-new house in Cypress, California, when our daughter started kindergarten. I was very involved with the children's school. I was a member of the PTA and volunteered in our son's classroom.

At this point in our marriage, life was perfect. We were secure and believed our marriage would last forever. We went to Spain in 1974, the same year my mother and father celebrated their fortieth wedding anniversary. Little did we know, ten years later, we would separate.

Our son's first-grade teacher recommended me for a position with the Regional Occupational Program. The program was part of the vocational education program for high school students and adults in the Anaheim School District. My job was located at Anaheim High School, and my official title was Assistant to the Career Guidance Counselor.

Everyone in the counseling office and the administrative staff were my mentors. Their encouragement enabled me to learn, grow, and discover talents and skills that I never recognized before. During that time, I organized a guest speaker program for the career center, counseled students, and wrote a vocational curriculum for the California Department of Education. My next assignment was as program director for an on-campus preschool. The high school students had an opportunity to receive elective credits while working in a preschool environment. There were about twelve high school students and fifteen preschool children in the program. My job was to lead planning sessions with the high school students; each session was designed to prepare them for the various tasks they would perform with the preschoolers. The high school students participating did the work, and I supervised.

During this time, I was attending Long Beach State College, taking classes to get my Para-Professional Vocational Educational Counseling Certificate. I graduated after two years; also during that time I worked in merchandising at Disneyland, as a summer employee. I was working at one of the shops in Adventureland. Working at Disneyland was fun; it truly is one of the happiest places in the world!

It is amazing how a little kindness and mentoring can change your life. Christ was both planting seeds of hope and preparing me for His purpose for my life. At the time, I had no idea that it was He who was opening the doors of opportunities for me to learn and grow, but these experiences shaped my future efforts for His kingdom. All the experiences that I had in counseling, teaching, mentoring, and administrative work were life-changing for me and it is these experiences that became the "talents" I would use in His service later in life. At times, I thought about bringing a cot to school and staying there. Returning home day after day in the afternoons was very painful, because I knew there would be no "Hi honey, how was your day?" waiting for me. Communication between my husband and I was nonexistent at this time in our marriage. Our family grew apart, and we each lived our own life. We were individuals busy with our own agendas. When married couples fail to communicate, it brings a lot of pain to the whole family.

Shortly after my daughter graduated from high school, she moved out and started working full-time. My husband and I had our jobs, and our son was wrapped up in high school varsity football (which was the best thing for him at the time).

I knew our marriage was in trouble, and I decided to go to a marriage and family counselor. My husband, though, refused to go. It takes two—both parties—to heal a marriage, and after three months of individual counseling, the counselor gave me the following evaluation: Irreconcilable differences and dysfunctional family environment learned by family of origin. Realizing our marriage didn't have a chance, and that I needed to heal and continue therapy, I decided to pursue a divorce. Our son graduated in June of 1983; my husband and I separated in January 1984. I believe that sometimes we need to experience life on our own terms to understand fully how much we need Christ in our life. This was that time for me.

Doing what you know in your heart is the right thing to do gives you hope for a better life. Learning and growing can be painful and exhilarating all rolled into one.

Starting over again as a single woman at age forty-three wasn't going to be easy. After moving into my own apartment, I remember thinking to myself: *There has to be a better way to live.* Jesus was listening; though, it would be many years later that I realized He had heard me.

CHAPTER TWO

THE LORD OPENS DOORS

C hrist was always with me, but I failed to notice Him during my childhood and young adult years. My life, until this point, was focused on survival not the Bible. Christ knew my heart, though, and He continually opened doors of opportunities and sent mentors, teachers, and friends— angels, really—to support me through life's valleys. As the Lord led me into a relationship with Him, my life completely turned around. Throughout the rest of the book, I tell the story of how the Lord led me to a relationship with Him.

Continuing my search for a better life, I started visiting a therapist who advised me to join a codependency support group. And thanks to the group's excellent instructor, I gained a wealth of knowledge. Codependency is like an addiction, and there are many codependent addicts. It takes a lot of self-control and therapy to heal from codependency. It is one of the hardest habits to break. Codependency can destroy relationships. This class helped me to see the truth about my own issues—like my need to always be accepted. My parents were unable to give me the kind of nurturing that every child needs, and the lack of love, acceptance, and a sense of belonging that I felt in my childhood affected most of my adult life. Thank heaven the Lord was patient with me, because change takes time and it doesn't come easy. At this point, all I wanted from life was to continue to grow and have peace. I started attending church at Crystal Cathedral in Garden Grove, California—where I started my faith journey. I realized that Christ was real, but it would take years for me to learn and grow my faith before I could call myself a Christian and to truly understand the meaning and reality of having a relationship with Him.

I met a man at Crystal Cathedral's singles group who was very kind to me. Over time, we started dating and attending church together. Through the inspiring message of Pastor Robert Schuller, Sr., and the encouragement of my friend, my faith was growing stronger. He was very kind and always made me laugh. He became my mentor and friend, and I was falling in love with him. It was hard to give him up, but I knew that God wanted me to turn to Him for healing. My divorce wasn't even final, and it was too soon for me to begin a serious relationship with anyone. We dated for six months before deciding to no longer see each other.

I missed our time together and was thankful that we remained friends and kept in touch. I will always consider him my friend. This was a difficult time for me. I was still negotiating my divorce settlement, and my children were busy with their own lives and were struggling to accept the divorce. My children and I got together only once a month and on holidays.

Added to this, I was a brand-new Christian struggling with life and trying to seek Christ on my own terms. Christ continued to walk beside me in this journey, but it took a long time for me to completely trust Him. I was like doubting Thomas in the Bible. In January 1986, my divorce was final. My job had changed, and I wasn't happy about the changes—my position was no longer challenging enough—so I decided to give my notice and start looking for a full-time position. Again, I turned to temporary job services to explore different companies and their work environments. I thought that one of my assignments might lead to a permanent position. What I really wanted to do was start my own business, but I didn't have a clue how, what, or where. Soon after my divorce was final, I decided to return to the Crystal Cathedral singles group on Tuesday nights. It was amazing how much the group had changed since I was last there. One night, when the group had taken a break I decided to go outside for a little fresh air. As I was standing by the door, an older gentleman walked toward me. We smiled at one another, and he introduced himself. "Hi, I'm Bob." He asked me if I planned to go dancing with the rest of the group after the meeting.

"I'll have to ask my friend."

Once the meeting was finished and the group dispersed, my girlfriend and I decided to join the group and go dancing. That night Bob asked me to dance with him. He was a great dancer, so we ended up dancing until the place closed. He asked me to dinner before we left, so I gave him my number and suggested he call.

The next day, he called to let me know he was traveling to Germany on business and would like to see me again before he left. We had a hard time picking a date; I was busy that month, but we managed, and he took me to a beautiful restaurant on the water in Long Beach. We had a table by a window with a breathtaking view of the historic Queen Mary, a ship originally built in Scotland that served in both world wars before retiring to Long Beach in 1967. The restaurant offered dancing during dinner, and we could see the fireworks show from the ship's deck. The date went so well, he asked me to go on another and asked me to choose the location. When I chose Disneyland, he acted a little surprised. I told him Disneyland offered dancing, too, and we could go on some fun rides. Hesitantly, he agreed. We had so much fun that we stayed until the park closed. At the end of the night, he said he was sad the night had to end.

After a couple more dates, Bob let me know he was leaving for Korea on another business trip. I took him to the airport before leaving for a cruise to Mexico with the athletic singles group I belonged to. When Bob returned from his overseas trip, we picked up right where we left off. Our relationship flourished; we enjoyed our dates and time together.

In 1984, I joined Soroptimist International, a professional businesswomen's organization. They were hosting a Halloween party, so Bob and I decided to attend as Harpo and the nurse. All my friends really got along well with Bob. As we were dancing, one of the songs that was playing was "Can I Have This Dance for the Rest of My Life." As we looked into each other's eyes, we knew we were falling in love. This would be the song we would play for our first dance at our wedding reception.

HARPO AND THE NURSE GOING TO HALLOWEEN PARTY

Neither Bob nor I planned to fall in love. I was newly divorced, and Bob had been single for thirteen years. Later on, we knew that it was God's divine plan for us to be together.

All the wonderful things that happened to Bob and me were gifts from the Lord. He blessed our life together so we, in turn, could bless others. I can't remember asking God for anything for myself, either before I became a Christian or after. I felt I needed to prove that I was worthy by seeking Him, learning, and growing as I continued my faith journey. I feel He blessed my life because I didn't ask.

The fall passed quickly, and Christmas was right around the corner. My children and a couple of their friends came over to decorate Bob's condominium for Christmas. Bob had a boat slip (one he was renting out) so we could use the little pier to watch the Huntington Harbor Christmas boat parade. After the children decorated, we all went out on the pier to watch the festively adorned boats motor by. I brought cookies and hot chocolate, and we all enjoyed our time together.

A couple of weeks before Christmas, Bob asked me to fly to Arizona the day after Christmas to meet his children. They decided to spend Christmas together, even his ex-wife was joining them. I asked him if he was sure he wanted me to meet his children at this time. "Yes," Bob said. His ex-wife was leaving the following day, and he wanted me to drive to Nevada with him and the children. Bob and his sister were having a ninetieth birthday party for their mother in Las Vegas. He thought this was a perfect time for me to meet the rest of the family. I had already met his mother, sister, and a few other members of the family, so I was looking forward to the trip. The children were very nice to me; I really enjoyed our time together. After meeting his children, I felt very secure about our future together.

Bob and I continued to attend the Crystal Cathedral to listen to Rev. Schuller's positive messages. He shared his experiences spreading the Gospel throughout the world.

> Crystal Cathedral's Mission Statement: "Find a need and fill it, find a hurt and heal it".

EASTER SUNDAY AT THE CRYSTAL CATHEDRAL

As Bob and I were growing in faith, we were learning how to turn our lives into something better than we dreamed possible. God was planting His seeds of hope in us. We joined a psychology/theology bible study group. Frank Freed, the instructor, was a family and marriage counselor.

We had many talks on Bob's patio in Huntington Harbor about our relationship, our faith, and our future hopes. If there were issues in our relationship I found difficult, I would ask him if we could talk, and we would head for the patio. He bought me a cup that read "Can We Talk?" We often discussed putting God in the center of our relationship, always continuing growing in our shared faith; and we would pray for our marriage and our families. Those talks cemented our relationship.

CHAPTER THREE

CELEBRATION OF
A NEW LIFE

The first year and a half, we grew together in faith and friendship; we fell in love and became soul mates.

Our relationship was full of lasting memories. We both loved the ocean and spent a lot of time at the beach, riding bikes, and eating dinners at our favorite restaurants. In March 1988, Bob asked me to marry him; He promised me a perpetual honeymoon. We picked out my engagement ring together (He wanted it that way.) Never did I dream that I could find someone that would love me as much as I loved him.

In April, on my birthday, I decided to go down to the beach by myself to thank the Lord for His many blessings. I had been smoking for thirty years and never could quit. I knew it bothered Bob, but he never asked me to quit. I decided to give myself a birthday present and quit smoking. It has been twenty-nine years since I smoked-another one of Christ's blessings.

We decided to marry in August at the Crystal Cathedral. The ceremony would be held in the Tower of Hope at the Chapel in The Sky, a small chapel on the twelfth floor. Since this was our second marriage, we decided to invite only family to the ceremony and afterward to celebrate with family and friends at a dinner with dancing at the Buena Park Hotel in Buena Park.

Several of the Soroptimist women gave me a bridal shower and played a big part in our wedding reception planning. There were so many women in the organization with business and talents. My best friend, Cleo, owed a beauty salon, so she did my hair for the wedding and agreed to oversee the reception to make sure everything went smoothly. One of the women owned a printing company and printed our invitations; another friend in the organization owned a flower shop where we ordered our flowers. One of the women helped me pick out my dress and another designed a matching wedding hat.

We had so much fun planning our wedding. We both looked forward to sharing our joy with friends and family. Our joy was noticeable. I will never forget Rob's (Bob's son) toast. He congratulated us and said that one of his observations during our courtship was "How we brought life to each other."

Christ planted seeds of love and blessed us. Our fairytale was just beginning. Everything I am about to share with you was a gift from the Lord. He showed us His awesome creation, through the Holy Spirit, and it became alive to us as we traveled.

A couple of our friends asked if we would like to spend a week in Mexico with them in September. If we chose to go, we would be one of four couples staying in two condominiums at a new Mexican resort. Our friend Linda was having her fiftieth birthday party, and they asked if we would like to have a duel celebration. We loved the idea of going to a place where there wouldn't be a lot of tourists.

We stayed in a little Mexican country beach town called Barra de Navidad. To get there, we had to fly into Guadalajara and travel by tour bus to our destination. We got to know all the locals. Very few tourists were in the area, so we were practically the only "gringos" in the whole town.

One Sunday morning, as we were going down a dirt road, we saw a group of children walking with the padre—the priest there. As we watched, they entered the church. Our curiosity got the best of us, so we decided to go inside to find out what was going on.

The children were sitting in pews, and the adults were standing next to the walls. In this little town, the children had their own church service. It was so heartwarming to see all these children listening to every word the padre said. He did skits with them and shared how Jesus would want them to treat each other. You could tell that their parents made sure that their children understood how important it was to go to church and learn about Jesus.

The time we spent in this little town celebrating with friends and getting to know the locals was meaningful for both of us. This little town—Barra de Navidad—was named after my favorite time of year—Christmas! We *really* hated to leave.

After our return from Mexico, we settled into our little condominium and continued to work and enjoy our life together. I helped Bob start a business, Marketing Plus International (M.P.I.), while we were dating, and it was a big part of our relationship. M.P.I. provided us the opportunity to work and continue our faith walk together. We stayed true to our faith and always sought to run our business with integrity, honesty, truth, and with a genuine concern for our customers, which are all God's principles. Because of this, I believe, God blessed the work of our hands (Psalm 90:17). We never knew when the Lord was going to show up. We were encouraged by Reverend Schuller's message on possibility thinking and to never give up on your dreams. My husband's business experience, hard work and help from Holy Spirit was the reason our business was a success.

We worked with major USA manufacturers to develop special markets and the sale of their products to mail-order catalogs, premium customers, and the internet.

The company was established in June 1987 and was also engaged as a marketing agent for several foreign companies, primarily in the photographic industry. We represented manufacturers who sold products in catalogs including Bookstone Solutions, National Geographic, Magellan, Sharper Image, and many others.

Every month, we travelled to a different part of the country: New York, Washington D.C., Florida, Georgia, New Orleans,

Dallas, and most of the western states. We were expected to attend manufacturers' sales meetings and conventions and to call on customers. At the peak of our business, we represented fifteen different manufacturers. We could handle most of the business on the road. My son would actually move into our house while we were away on trips. This was a major help to us. He would make sure we knew what was happening at home, and he let us know what needed to be done. My daughter was a backup for us, if my son wasn't available.

CARRIAGE RIDE THROUGH CENTRAL PARK

Bob's sister died in May 1989, and my first grandchild was born the same day. That was a bittersweet day for us. Bob was *very* close to his sister, yet I felt so blessed to be with my daughter when she gave birth to Tyler, my first grandson. It was love at first sight. During the first five years of his life, he spent a lot of time with us. I couldn't keep my hands off of him; he was such a sweet baby.

After Bob's sister died, his mother moved from Las Vegas, Nevada, to her granddaughter's (Bob's sister's daughter) home in El Cajon, California. She was ninety-three.

We felt we needed a bigger place, knowing that his mother would be staying with us, and we wanted to accommodate other family members who came to visit. We found a condominium in a great community in Irvine with more space. A small lake was within walking distance.

CHAPTER FOUR

THE STORY OF US

We spent the first few years establishing M.P.I.
After we moved to Irvine, our faith and business
really started to grow. We made our decisions
based on possibility thinking: "I can do all things through
him who gives me strength." (Philippians 4:13).

Everyone wondered how the two of us ran the business
ourselves. I told them we placed Christ at the center of our
personal and professional life; He also gave us the gift of
organization. Attending Crystal Cathedral and the adult
Bible classes kept us centered on our faith journey.

Our first trip to Europe together was in September, 1993.
We flew to England to meet with Bob's business associate. We
toured London, then decided to take the train north. We rented
a car and drove to Warwick Castle. The castle, built in Saxton
medieval times, had been transformed into a beautiful mansion,
but the dungeon there was a reminder of its long eventful history.

We were only minutes away from Stratford-Upon-Avon—
Shakespeare's birth place. We settled into The Sequoia House,
a bed and breakfast within walking distance of the town, River
Avon, and the Royal Shakespeare Theatre. The theatre was right
on the River Avon. The next night we decided to walk over to

the theatre to see a play: *The Merry Wives of Windsor.* The walk back was a romantic one. Lights danced on the water as we crossed the little bridge that led back to our bed and breakfast. Holding hands, we sat on a bench, and I thanked Jesus for putting in our hearts His unconditional love that we shared.

SEQUOIA HOUSE STRATFORD ON AVON, ENGLAND

The next day we drove to the English Channel to catch the Jetfoil (a passenger carrying waterjet) to Belgium, and from there we caught a train to Cologne, Germany, to work.

Every two years, the International Photo Show was in Cologne. Bob and I attended business meetings during the day and dinner parties and meetings at night. Bob was so considerate. Most of the people attending the meetings were men, and Bob always introduced me as his wife and business partner.

BUSINESS DINNER MEETING IN COLOGNE

I didn't attend all the meetings, choosing instead to rest and tour. One of the hotel hostesses helped me make tour plans. She even walked me over to her hair salon. The hair stylist there could not speak English, so she explained how I wanted my hair done and told me how much it would cost in German money.

We finished our work in Cologne, and our next stop was southern Germany's Black Forest. We stayed in a castle right in the middle of a lush green forest. The castle had a real drawbridge and was just like something out of a fairy tale. It felt like a dream, one from which I did not want to wake. This trip to Europe was the start of our perpetual honeymoon.

The next day we headed for Vienna, Austria. We stayed at a hotel within walking distance of shopping and the Vienna Opera House. We had dinner at an outside café and walked to the opera house. The performance was all the beautiful music for which Austria is famous. As we were walking back to our hotel, I was thinking that this time and place would be with me in memory always.

We continued our journey, stopping at Innsbruck and Salzburg in Austria; we visited as many churches as time would allow along the way. We always prayed for our family, and I thanked God for watching over us as we traveled.

We stayed at a bed and breakfast in Rinn, Austria. Our room was on the second floor with a view of the mountains and miles of beautiful open country. Part of the movie *The Sound of Music* was filmed in this area.

VIEW FROM ROOM AT THE B&B IN RINN

The next day, we were on the road again to Lake Como, Italy, where the wealthy own large lake villas. We stayed in one of the villa's that had been converted into a hotel.

VIEW OF LAKE COMO, IN ITALY

We dined at a beautiful restaurant overlooking the lake and left the next morning for Milan to fly home. The trip was wonderful. We travelled to Europe every September for the next four years—sometimes for business and sometimes for pleasure. Upon arriving home in California, we had two and half weeks of mail to sort through—there was a lot of work to catch up on. It was good to be home; I really missed our family. We continued to work hard and travel. Our favorite song was "On The Road Again."

You might think this story I am sharing with you is too much like a fairy tale to be true, but all things are possible to those who believe. There is nothing in the world that can compare with the Lord's love. Christ gave us grace, forgiveness, and love for one other. He equipped us with the strength, creativity, and wisdom to run our business.

I was asked if I wanted to volunteer at a shelter for battered women, and I was happy to say, "Yes!" It had always been my heart's desire to mentor women that had been abused, either verbally or physically. After spending a month in training, I decided to volunteer to teach women to explore different career opportunities. I found that most of the women were so traumatized that they wouldn't be able to hold down any job. I told the counselors that they needed self-esteem and life skills classes, so they could be confident enough to apply for a job. Knowing my previous background, they asked me if I would volunteer to teach the class at the shelter on a regular basis. Little did I know that this would be God's purpose for my life. It finally dawned on me that Christ really wanted my heart.

I realized that my desire to reach out to others, had to be the Holy Spirit working in my heart. Through His love, He was leading me to my destiny.

Bob was asked to be a New Hope phone counselor at Crystal Cathedral. Once he committed, he was trained by the church psychiatrist. I was able to take the same classes, because of my volunteer work at the battered women's shelter. Bob took calls from all over the world. The Crystal Cathedral service was broadcasted in many different countries. Bob and I serving the Lord together brought so much joy to our lives. The Lord continued to fill our hearts with love for each other. Never did I dream that life could be so wonderful.

Simultaneously volunteering at the shelter and serving as vice president of our own business was a challenge. Added to these responsibilities, finding time for our relationship, church, and families was important to us. Success was possible through organization and prioritizing our schedules.

Believe it or not, we did have time for fun activities; we enjoyed dancing, performing arts, playing cards, fun picnics and concerts at the lake with our family, birthday parties for the grandchildren in our backyard, and of course, traveling. We stayed focused on our faith, giving Christ the glory for our many blessings, and the love of friends and family.

For our ten-year wedding anniversary we decided to renew our vows at our home. We wanted to share our happiness with our friends and family. A few days before the celebration, a good friend of ours died suddenly at age fifty-nine. Linda and her husband were to attend our anniversary party. The family didn't remember the exact date of our anniversary, and they held the funeral on the same day.

This was hard on everyone that knew Linda. We had belonged to the same Soroptomist organization, and she and her husband were one of the couples who we travelled to Mexico with. It was a sad time for all of us.

We renewed our vows about a month following her funeral. We were glad that Linda's husband and their son were able to join us. One of the Crystal Cathedral pastor's performed the ceremony; he was also a good friend. My grandson was ring bearer, and my granddaughter was the flower girl. We lit a candle in memory of Linda.

The most memorable part of the celebration was the following poem my husband wrote to me:

IT STARTED WITH A SMILE

*It all started with a little smile And lasted more than
just a little while what has followed is a story to be
told of activities and memories to behold
It seemed appropriate to tie the knot insuring the "perpetual
honeymoon" will never stop. The family gathered at the tower
in the sky and witnessed sanctification by the man on high.
The Mexican honeymoon with friends so dear gave the
union a great start, its first year Many fun times were
enjoyed from then on to far-away places even across the
pond There was New York where not by choice
A show blossomed for the boys by Joyce And Hawaii when
snorkeling at Napili Bay a set of keys were picked up by a wave
As business beckoned in northern climes Monterey proved to be
one of the best of times Then off to meet the Rodaway Clan
where Harpo and the nurse got quite a hand
Germany, England, Italy, Austria too
were very special where time really flew who could forget quaint
Whately Hall where among all the history a ghost did call
There were cruises of which there was much to see
The Mexican most memorable, the suite being the key
The Eastern Caribbean followed in the Spring of 94
Where our stable or horses made a big score
1997 was a vintage year, for a lady so dear as we
shared with our family mom's 100th year
While cruising was out, we did get about Denver and New
Orleans do standout So now we celebrate ten years of bliss
and the many fun things that were on our list Giving blessings to God
for making us mates and asking for more years to share our fates.
With much love from your best friend*

Crystal Cathedral announced that they were planning
a Holy Land tour from December 15 to December 26,
1999. The itinerary, along with the professional tour
company, made this a once-in-a-lifetime opportunity.

My father passed away in October that year, so we had to decide whether or not to go. My daughter agreed to be with my mom during Christmas, so we decided to go. We were given a replica of the oil lamp used in the Holy Land during the lifetime of Jesus. We bought several other lamps for our families to light on Christmas Eve.

CHAPTER FIVE

TRIP TO THE HOLY LAND

After boarding the bus that would take us to the airport, we prayed for travel mercy as a group. Finally, after many security checks, we boarded our plane. While we were taxiing down the runway, we noticed two police cars—one on the left wing and one on the right— following us. Security was tight, and there were concerns about Holy Land tours during the turn of the millennium.

After a long flight, we landed in Tel Aviv and boarded a bus to the Galilee Beach Hotel. Here, the view of the sea shore was spectacular. As Bob and I watched the sunset over the water's edge, we both felt an incredible peace, a peace so complete, I felt it deep in my soul.

I didn't realize that the Sea of Galilee was only twelve miles long by seven miles wide. It was here that Jesus walked on water (Mark 6:48-50).

The next day, we started our tour early in the morning. Our first stop was Tabgha, which was located on the northwestern shore of the Sea of Galilee. Jesus's fourth resurrection appearance after His crucifixion was in Tabgha. We visited a church there which was the approximate location were Jesus feed the multitudes in Matthew 14:19-21.

Our next destination was Mount of Beatitudes, the site of Jesus's famous Sermon on the Mount in Matthew 5. This beautiful spot was north of the Sea of Galilee. As we listened to the beatitudes, I was heavily affected by "Blessed are those who mourn, for they will be comforted" (Matthew 5:4). My father had passed away only a few months prior, and I cried for twenty-four hours afterward. I woke up the next morning, and my face was so swollen that I could hardly open my eyes. As I looked in the mirror, I heard my dad say, "You have grieved enough. You need to take care of your mother and prepare for a funeral." I am not sure if the voice was my dad or my heavenly Father.

The entire time we toured Israel, I felt the Lord's love. He was helping me heal and giving me His peace; I felt a transformation. I knew I would never be the same after this experience.

Capernaum was our next tour stop. Jesus made his home in Capernaum after John was arrested; from here, He would travel and preach.

We were *very* fortunate to have a professional guide. Every morning we met at eight to begin a new all-day tour. Everywhere we went, our guide shared in detail all the Biblical events of the area. Even more, the historical sites we visited were located close to our hotel, so we covered a lot of territory in a day.

We visited the Golan Heights. Because of its high elevation (it's near the Syrian border), the vantage points were breathtaking. Many soldiers have died in battles fought in this area. Israel needed this site to protect its people.

Cana is known for Jesus's first public miracle; here He turned water into wine at a wedding celebration (John 2:110). We all gathered at a little church, and one of the ministers touring with us, asked if there were any couples who would like to renew their wedding vows to please stand. This vow renewal ceremony was very moving for those of us who participated. This was the third time Bob and I exchanged vows. Our next stop was the Jordan River, where John the Baptist baptized Jesus. Yardenit Baptismal was the site where tourists visiting the Holy Land could be baptized. Everyone in our tour changed into white gowns and were baptized. To be baptized in the same river as Jesus was an unforgettable experience. Just to be in the Jordan River was humbling. There were buildings surrounding the area where the baptisms were taking place. It wasn't like being out in the wilderness.

Sailing on the Sea of Galilee in antique boats was another moving experience. The sea was so calm—it looked like glass; then, we witnessed a perfect sunset. I felt as calm as the water looked, and I thought to myself that this may be a little of how it feels to be in heaven with the Lord.

The next day, we checked out of our hotel and departed for Jerusalem—the city of David. We stopped in Nazareth on the way, where the angel Gabriel told Mary that she would conceive and give birth to God's son (Luke 1: 30-33).

We checked into the Jerusalem Hyatt hotel, and for the next seven days, this place was our home. The following are historical highlights of Jerusalem and a few personal experiences of my time there:

- Jesus entered Jerusalem on Palm Sunday (Mark 11:1-11).
- Just before He was arrested, Jesus went to Gethsemane, at the foot of the Mount of Olives, and prayed (Mark 14:26-42).
- Bobby Schuller (Robert H. Schuller's Grandson) read scripture at some of the sights. Bobby was nineteen and had given his heart to the Lord.
- The ancient wall that surrounds Jerusalem has eight gates, one more was added later. The Golden Gate was sealed by the Muslims many years ago, and the other seven gates lead to different quarters of the old city, the Christian, Armenian, Jewish, and Muslim Quarters.
- The Church of the Holy Sepulchre is located close to the Christians' quarters. The Via Dolorosa (meaning the "way of sorrow" housing the fourteen "stations of the cross") is on a path outside the church. This is where Christ carried the cross on which He would be crucified. Being in Jerusalem gave me a feeling of sadness. No one could ever imagine the pain that Christ must have suffered during His scourging, carrying of the cross, and crucifixion.
- The Garden Tomb is located outside the city walls. The door to the tomb had a sign that read: He is not here— For He Has Risen. As I walked in the tomb, I thanked God and Christ for their sacrifice. The Garden outside the tomb was beautiful, the birds were chirping as the pastor read scripture by the empty tomb (John 20:110). After the scripture was read, we all took communion. Never in my life did I ever feel so loved and peaceful. I thought about His amazing grace and mercy. It was hard for me to imagine the love that God feels for us. To sacrifice His son for our sins.
- The Western Wall, known to many as the Wailing Wall, symbolizes the return of the people of Israel to the Holy Land of Promise. It is a sacred shrine for the Jewish people and a place for public worship and celebration. Some wrote their prayers on a small piece of paper and

slipped them into the cracks in the wall. I wrote a special prayer for family members that had heavy burdens.

- A visit to the Dead Sea natural health facilities, where guests can get into big vats of mud (with bathing suits) and cover each other with mud and be kids again, was our next stop. You let the mud dry and then rinse off in showers. Then float in the thermo-mineral water bathes.

- Masada was our next stop. Masada is a mountain fortress located on the eastern edge of the Judean Desert, overlooking the Dead Sea. To get to Masada you must ride a Gondola. This was the site that Herod built his magnificent palace. After Jerusalem was destroyed in A.D. 70, a group of Jewish rebels known as Zealots encamped in the safety of this fortress. They managed to hold off the Roman forces for three years. When they couldn't hold off the Romans any longer, they decided to commit a mass suicide rather than be captured.

- After much prayer for an end to Israel's drought, it rained on Christmas Eve night in Bethlehem. Michael Crawford flew in just for that night and sang "Oh Little Town of Bethlehem" and "Silent Night." We had small flash lights that lit up the sky. As the rain came down on my face, I knew Christ's presence. I never felt closer to Christ than at that moment.

The group that were part of the service were the first to get out of the rain; our group came next. Michael Crawford was standing at the door and said to me, "Wasn't that incredible?" I didn't know what to say, I came out with a weak "Yes." His voice is God's gift to him and he shared it with us! Someone in our group took a picture of the two of us together.

On Christmas Day, our minister gave an inspirational message about peace for the millennium. We had a nice brunch before we prepared for our trip home. A few people in our group met later that afternoon to talk about highlights of our trip. Each of us shared a prayer to Jesus about our experience. As we were flying home from this amazing trip, I was thinking about our travels through Israel. To be where Jesus was and to share our faith with fellow Christians was an incredible experience and blessing. My overall feelings while we were there, were sadness, compassion, humbleness, love, joy, peace, and hope.

CHAPTER SIX

A LIFE-CHANGING MOVE

Two years after we returned from Israel, Bob's mother passed away. She was 104 years old. Bob and I were fortunate to have our mothers with us for as long as we did. We have many good memories of the time we spent with them. Bob's mother lived with Judy, Bob's niece and her husband, Aubrey. Bob and I visited for a couple of weeks every other month to give them a break. Mom was a kind soul, our family misses her.

In 2001 Bob and I decided it was a good time for us to move to our Boulder City condominium (which we had paid off) and were renting out. The condominium was tri-level with a lovely view of Lake Mead from the living room. We were semi-retired and considering retiring full time.

I informed the battered women's shelter that we planned to move a few weeks before Christmas. They threw a goingaway Christmas party for me just before we moved.

The women asked me to promise to continue the program, if at all possible. They all shared the belief that many women need this type of program. I thought it might be a good idea to ask for letters of recommendation, in case there might be an opportunity to continue. The following are the letters of recommendations from the counselors and director of the shelter:

To Whom It May Concern: 11-29-01

Joyce Lewis aka Dr. Joyce, a nickname that the women in her group gave her, was cheerful, resourceful and was knowledgeable about the subject matter. She never stops smiling; the residents loved her groups as they would take turns to speak and discuss their issues while they were getting individual attention in a group setting; they also appreciated her honesty. Everyone who gets to know her will become engaged in a positive sense of the world around.

Shelter Supervisor

2nd letter
To Whom it May Concern: 11/30/2001

Joyce Lewis has conducted a weekly group on self-esteem/ life skill classes for women for the last five years. Over the time she has been here she has been more than just a group leader. Her groups have been very inspirational for the women, giving them hope and support beyond the usual scope of our groups. She is beloved and respected by all of the women in the shelter, and once they graduate they are eager to return to the meetings she holds for graduates.

Lead Counselor

3rd letter
To Whom It May Concern: 1/30/2001

Joyce Lewis has been a dedicated, hard-working volunteer. She is empathetic and truly cares for the women in her group. She has a genuine soft style, which creates an ideal atmosphere for growth and learning. The participants in her groups truly enjoyed and have benefited from them.

Shelter Program Director

<u>Group Participants' Comments:</u>
*"You have brought so much sunshine and brightness to
our group. Your gift of yourself and your workshops/information
have meant so much to me. You have opened my eyes to all
the potential having good self-esteem can accomplish."*
*"I've learned so much out of our meetings, these past
months. I thank God for sending you to us, your girls."*
"Please keep in touch. We'll miss you so much in our lives."
"You have opened my mind and heart to a better way of thinking."

Christ put it on my heart to share my testimony with the
women at the battered women's shelter; it was not my plan. I was
not allowed to quote scripture or talk about faith. But the women
understood that my faith was strong. After a few sessions with
them, I knew God's purpose for my life was to mentor women who
have been emotionally abused. All the kind things that everyone
said about me was really because of Christ's love. When the Lord
fills your heart with love, you can't keep it to yourself. He planted
his seeds of hope and love in me so that I could pass it on to others.

"For I know the plans I have for you," declares the
Lord, "plans to prosper you and not to harm you, plans to
give you hope and a future." Then you will call on me and
I will listen to you. You will seek me and find me when
you seek me with all your heart (Jeremiah 29:11-13).

I was apprehensive about moving to a small town in the
middle of the desert, but after we became acquainted with the
people in Boulder City, we found it to be a very friendly town.
People made time to be friendly and helpful. The former mayor
of Boulder City Bob Ferraro would stop and chat with you, if
he passed you on the street. Mayor Bob was part of the City
Council for thirty-one years, six terms as mayor, and the rest
of the time he served on the board; he retired in 2007. I was
curious about his background and was thankful when he agreed
to an interview. He grew up in a Paradise Valley, a small northern
Nevada ranching community, Bob was often the only student
in his class. He attended the University of Nevada Reno (UNR)

and graduated in 1957. After college, he went to Pakistan for two years as a U.S. State Department agricultural liaison and later traveled the world logging more than 100,000 miles while visiting sixty-six countries during his thirty-year engineering career with American Pacific Corporation. One of the perks of being mayor, he said, was serving on the Civilian Military Counseling Board at Nellis Air Force Base. He was asked to copilot both the F-15 and F-16. Bob and his wife Connie have dedicated a big portion of their life together to the people of Boulder City.

In 2003, I was invited to join Philanthropic Educational Organization (P.E.O.). The organization was founded in 1869 by several young women. They formalized a college sorority on the campus of Iowa Wesleyan College. Theirs was a pioneer and rigorous background with highly significant emphasis on education. These were new concepts in a century just awakening to the tremendous possibilities involved in educating women.

Note: Reference to PEO Founders Booklet.

The P.E.O. mission statement is: Promoting Educational opportunities for women. Our sisterhood proudly makes a difference in women's lives with six philanthropies that include Cottey College, and independent, liberal arts and sciences college for women, and five programs that provide higher educational assistance: Educational Loan Fund, International Peace Scholarship Fund, Program for Continuing Education, Scholar Awards and Star Scholarship. P.E.O. is headquartered in Des Moines, Iowa.

All the members have talents and gifts. Being a part of the PEO has inspired me to continue to grow. I cherish the friendships that I have made through the years. We all try to support each other through the good times and bad.

Bob and I still have our business, but haven't been traveling as much. Most of the conventions that we attended were at the convention center in Las Vegas, thirty miles away. Our business was steady, because we had repeat customers. I guess you could say that we were semi-retired.

We would sit on our patio and have coffee in the mornings. The view of the lake was beautiful. We talked about all the sailboats on the lake and how much fun it would be to sail there.

One Sunday, Lake Mead Marina had a boat fair. Thirty boats that were on display, and the owners were there to negotiate pricing. We found our sailboat that day—a twenty-seven-foot McGregor; it slept four comfortably, had small bathroom, stove, refrigerator, plenty of sitting room, and speakers inside and out. The engine was powerful enough for us to easily motor, if we didn't want to sail. After negotiating the price, we bought the boat and rented a slip at the marina.

After making the purchase, we met the local sailing club, a group of sailors who met once a month. Most of the people in the group were serious sailors who liked to have fun. They would schedule races, have pool parties, camp in the mountains during the summer time, and take weekend sailing trips to places on the lake. I affectionately called them our boatpeople friends. They were like family to us. They were always available to help us, if we needed it. Also we learned a lot about sailing from the group. Bob had some experience, but I didn't, so we both took sailing lessons. Our boat, which we named "Serenity," was another one of Christ's gifts. We will never forget our sailing family and sharing our Lake Mead adventures with friends and family.

Our Sailing Boat "Serenity"

More and more I was falling in love with Boulder City and its open spaces, sunsets, and, of course, the beautiful moon over the lake. On a clear night hundreds of stars were visible. I never thought I would love living in the desert, but I was wrong.

In November 2009, Bob's former boss Jack Hannes invited us to travel to Sydney, Australia, to spend a week with him and his wife Margaret. Jack was owner of Hanimex International Camera Company, and Bob was President of Hanimex USA operations before I met him. Jack was turning eighty and wanted to have a reunion with the Hanimex former employees and to celebrate his birthday at the same time. They had a beautiful home on Sydney bay. It was a three-story home with an elevator, swimming pool, dock, and speed boat. The house had a spectacular view of the water. Jack took us out to lunch at a restaurant on the harbor in his speedboat. We had a wonderful time visiting Jack and Margaret. They were such gracious hosts.

Kangaroo Park, outside of Sydney

The last night we were in Sydney, we stayed at hotel—the location of the reunion and birthday—on the outskirts of the City. I met many people who attended the party through our business connections. Bob enjoyed reconnecting with many of the people he had worked with over the years, and everyone had a great time.

The next day, we flew to Cairns. Jack made hotel reservations for us, and arranged a barrier reef tour by boat the next day. Out in the middle of the sea were huge flat platforms the size of a small island. We snorkeled on one side of the platform, and on the other side was an underwater observation room to view the beautiful sea creatures and fish. We ate lunch and enjoyed ourselves the rest of the day. There were helicopter platforms not too far from where we were. Helicopters brought tourists in for afternoon scuba diving excursions.

We had a full day and were ready to return to dry land! We had dinner and went to bed early.

The next day we were off to the rainforest. Not far from Cairns, was the Skyrail Rainforest Cableway. There, we boarded what resembled old passenger trains and were blessed by sights of lush green forest and waterfalls. After leaving the train, we had the opportunity to take the cable car across the rainforest—the view was breathtaking. At the center of the rainforest, the cable stopped to give us a chance to explore. The scenery—beautiful trees and plants along with magnificent flowers in vibrant colors—made a picturesque setting. We took the sky-rail to the train and made it back to Cairns in time for dinner.

We took an early flight to our next adventure, Alice Springs, the location of Ayers Rock. The aboriginals consider Ayers Rock sacred ground and one of the wonders of the world. The rock is one of the world's largest monoliths and Australia's most visited site. There we had a sunset picnic with champagne and grilled hot dogs. As the sun sets, the rock's appearance changes from red to many colors. We met interesting people from all over the world. Everyone was friendly and appreciated being in this part of the world; it is truly one of God's wonders.

After we returned to Alice Springs, we stopped by a local store for water, and were surprised by a man's appearance at the store. He looked like he'd been hit by a truck, so we asked him what happened. He was driving on the open road in the desert, and he was unable to avoid a camel that ran across the road. His rental car was totaled. That poor man was just like us, on vacation from the United States. We had no idea that Australia had camels that ran wild in the desert.

The next night we went to an aboriginal cultural experience; a traditional and contemporary artist shared aboriginal stories around a large fire. There was also cultural dancing. (I actually got to dance with the performers!) It was fun to be in a different country and to interact with its people through their native culture. The food was delicious, too. We returned to Sydney the next day, where we spent the night, before flying home to the good ol' USA.

This was another perpetual honeymoon we will never forget. God is always there to watch over us and to give us safe travel.

There is one more trip I have to share with you. For my sixty-fifth birthday, my husband gave me a trip to Rome. Before we left, he bought a compact disc of Italian love songs.

We stayed in a small suite on the fifth floor of the Hilton in the hills, a beautiful place that overlooked Rome and the Vatican. From our balcony, we could see the Vatican and the city. There was a celebration while we were there, and one evening, just before we left for my birthday dinner, a fireworks display lit the sky over the Vatican. The view from our balcony was perfect. Bob turned to me and said, "I arranged the fireworks just for your special birthday."

Fireworks over the Vatican from our balcony

Bob arranged breakfast to be brought to us the next morning on a rolling table. Two days later, we boarded a cruise ship leaving to cruise the Italian Rivera for eleven days. We started in Rome and continued on to Florence, Pompeii, Dubrovnik, Monaco, Monte Carlo, Venice, and more. After returning to Rome, we flew to Zurich, Switzerland. I had never been there, so Bob thought that I should see it while we were in Europe. This was truly an amazing perpetual honeymoon trip. It couldn't have been more perfect. I was on cloud nine for weeks afterward.

As we continued to keep Christ at the center of our life, He continued to open doors of opportunity. He poured His incredible grace, mercy, love, and blessings on us. So we could share the message in the Gospel with others.

CHAPTER SEVEN

TRANSITIONS MINISTRY AT CENTRAL CHRISTIAN CHURCH

We attended Central Christian Church the first time on Christmas Eve 2001. We were brand new to Nevada, having been there only a couple of weeks. There was a skit at the service that day about people spending their first Christmas in the desert. We knew this service was just for us, and we had found our church.

Soon after we began attending church, Pastor Steve Cuss shared that Central was in need of a support group leader to minister to emotionally abused women. Of course, his plea touched my heart. The women at the shelter had asked me to continue my classes, and God certainly didn't waste time opening another door. God knew my heart for abused women. I had found my purpose; my trials became a testimony to use for His glory.

Pastor Steve and I met to discuss the possibility of starting a women's support group and how the church would support this effort by providing curriculum and leadership classes. He presented the idea to Central's administrators and leaders, and they agreed to let me have a room on Tuesday nights.

I named the support group Transitions. This was the start of the Lord transitioning many women to Christianity and then into a new life, through the Holy Spirit. Transitions' mission was to connect women to Christ by demonstrating that His love and His compassion strengthens us. The program was designed to motivate women to free themselves from controlling relationships by understanding self-esteem and the importance of healthy boundaries, according to scripture. Ours was a nine-week program. Transitions continued for eleven years at Central. The topics covered included an introductory week followed by workshops and discussion on self-esteem, codependent behavior, boundaries, emotions, toxic people, and we made time for guest speakers and a review session to offer participants information on how to continue their faith journey after they completed the program. Below are the guidelines and summaries of Transitions classes along with some of my thoughts:

Guidelines and Summaries of Transitions Classes

Transitions Objective

One objective of Transitions is to grow in faith by continually seeking a relationship with Christ: Are we walking down the same street, falling in the same hole and expecting different results? Are we committed to Christ, striving to stay on the path of faith, or do we have one foot on the dock and one in the boat? Do we stay faithful when it works for us, and when it doesn't do we go back to our old ways of thinking? When we go back to doing things our way, we drift and when things go wrong we have no anchor to hold on too. Christ will be with us through our healing, if we continue to seek him. Our Lord is the only one that can give us the strength to overcome the pain that we have gone through.

Transitions is about taking the plank out of our own eye and healing. This class is not about judging or trying to fix others. We are here to center ourselves in faith and to heal, keeping Christ at the center of our group.

Program Classes Self-Esteem

But the fruit of the Spirit is love, joy, peace, forbearance, kindness, goodness, faithfulness, gentleness and self-control. Against such things there is no law. Those who belong to Christ Jesus have crucified the flesh with its passions and desires.—Galatians 5:22-24

Healthy self-esteem is the eternal reality of who we are in Christ according to scripture. Jesus loves us and wants the best for us. He paid the price and died on the cross for our sins. All He wants from us is to have a loving relationship with Him and to learn the truth of the Gospel; If we do this, the Holy Spirit will enter our hearts and help us navigate through the time we are here on earth.

Codependent Behavior

Do not deceive yourselves. If any of you think you are wise by the standards of this age, you should become fools so that you may become wise.—1 Corinthians 3:18

Codependents seem to always be preoccupied with problems of others.

They also can be obsessed with controlling other people, by telling them how to solve their problems.

They try to manipulate others to do or feel the way they think is appropriate.

Agreeing with people so they won't feel rejected. Codependents put other people's needs over their own.

Instructor's comments: There is a lot of dysfunctional behavior in this world. To many people select their own reality based on their feelings at the time, which becomes their truth. Feelings are fleeting and can change very quickly. If we truly believe the Gospel, then we will realize that Jesus is the truth, the way, and the light. As we continue to seek a relationship with Him, He will give us His wisdom, strength, and courage when we are ready to really receive it. He will help us overcome the challenges of this world, through the Holy Spirit.

Boundaries

Put on the whole armor of God, so that you can take your stand against the devil's schemes. Flesh and blood, but against the evil rulers and the spiritual forces of evil in the heavenly realm, that have powers over this dark world. Therefore put on the full armor of God so that when the day of evil comes, you may be able to stand your ground, and after you have done everything, to stand. Stand firm then, with the belt of truth buckled around your waist, with the breastplate of righteousness in place.—Ephesians 6:11-14

Boundaries define us. The most basic boundary setting word is "no." This lets people know that we are in control of ourselves. We also need to be able to say no to ourselves. Selfcontrol is a very important part of boundaries. As we learn and grow in faith we become secure and confident about setting boundaries as we receive guidance from the Holy Spirit. The more vulnerable we are, the more we need to extend our boundaries.

<u>Instructors Comments</u>: In this lesson we were all learning together that we all needed help with boundaries. We discovered that walking in faith and communicating with Christ can heal us and give us a better understanding of the changes we needed to make.

Emotions

The Lord is my shepherd, I lack nothing. He makes me lie down in green pastures, he leads me beside quiet waters, he refreshes my soul. He guides me along the right paths for his name's sake.

Even though I walk through the darkest valley, I will fear no evil, for you are with me; your rod and your staff, they comfort me.

You prepare a table before me in the presence of my enemies. You anoint my head with oil; my cup overflows. Surely your goodness and love will follow me all the days of my life, and I will dwell in the house of the Lord forever.—Psalm 23

The self-esteem, codependency, and boundaries classes are important to learn how to establish good relationships; but equally as important in relationships is our emotional health. Emotions are often the driving force behind motivation, positive or negative.

The Bible gives us a clear path to follow. A healthy selfimage is seeing yourself as God sees you, no more or no less." Following God's message to us, gives us a road map to emotional security.

Instructors Comments: As the class felt comfortable enough to share, we discussed our emotional insecurities and looked to scripture for God's words for healing. This gave us the motivation to continue staying on the path to becoming a new creation in Christ. I had printouts from different sources on the subject of emotions. Most of the resources used were tools to help us heal from our negative emotions that we had been carrying around for years.

Guest Speaker

Week six of the Transitions program was reserved for guest speakers. We invited Central counselors and other group leaders to share their testimonies or speak on one of the week's subjects. We always included social time afterward with time for the women to ask questions.

Self-Talk

If we meditate on Christ's word, we will know the truth, and the truth shall set us free.—John 8:32)

This session covered the reality that our negative thinking toward Christ comes from Satan. He is the static that gets into our heads and our hearts. As believers, we must stay strong and continue to seek the truth that is found in the Gospel.

The Gospel is Christ's word to all people. Written by human authors under the guidance of the Holy Spirit, it is the supreme source of truth for Christian believers. Consider these scriptures:

- "Give careful thought to the paths for your feet and be steadfast in all your ways" Proverbs 4:26.
- Finally, brothers and sisters, whatever is true, whatever is noble, whatever is right, whatever is pure, whatever is lovely, whatever is admirable if anything is excellent or praiseworthy think about such things. Whatever you have learned or received or heard from me or seen in me put it into practice. And the God of peace will be with you" (Philippians 4: 8-9).
- For God so loved the world that he gave his one and only Son, that whoever believes in him shall not perish but have eternal life. For God did not send his son into the world to condemn the world, but to save the world" (John 3: 16-17).

As we continue to study scripture and grow in faith, we will have a better understanding of God's unconditional love for us.

Toxic People

Listen to my words, Lord, consider my lament.

Hear my cry for help, my King and my God, for to you I pray. In the morning, Lord, you hear my voice; in the morning I lay my requests before you and wait expectantly. For you are not a God who is pleased with wickedness; evil people cannot stand in your presence. You hate all who do wrong; you destroy those who tell lies. The bloodthirsty and deceitful you, Lord, detest. But I, by your great love, can come into your house; in reverence I bow down toward your holy temple. Lead me, Lord, in your righteousness because of my enemies—make your way straight before me.

Not a word from their mouth can be trusted;
their heart is filled with malice. Their throat is an
open grave; with their tongues they tell lies.

Declare them guilty, O God! Let their intrigues be their downfall.
Banish them for their many sins, for they have rebelled against you.

But let all who take refuge in you be
glad; let them ever sing for joy.

Spread your protection over them, that those who love your
name may rejoice in you. Surely, Lord, you bless the righteous; you
surround them with your favor as with a shield.— Psalm 5:1-12

Toxic people drain you mentally and spiritually. They have gigantic egos and they think they are always right. Their behavior is abusive, and they have no respect for anyone. If you work for or are married to a toxic person, they can make your life miserable. If you have ever had any kind of a relationship with a toxic person, you know what I am talking about. The good news is that nothing is impossible with Christ; by His grace He can change toxic people. Pray to the Lord for His wisdom on how to handle these people. Pray also for their salvation. Read the Psalm 5 to get a better perspective on how David prayed to the Lord about his enemies.

Instructors Comments: All of the women could relate to toxic people. As we studied scripture; we all realized how important it is to have a relationship with Christ for wisdom and strength. We reviewed the class curriculum and discussed: "Where Do We Go from Here?" Some of the women wanted to take the classes over again. They felt that this class was something they needed to continue to heal.

Many women stayed in the Transitions group for years. I provided leadership training classes for the women who remained, and these women eventually started a group they titled the Transformation Group, taken from Romans 12:2: "Do not conform to the pattern of this world, but be transformed by the renewing of your mind." They took turns leading faith-based curriculum studies. All of these women were amazing, and we learned a lot from each other. The Transformation leaders were my

Transitions co-leaders. When new people finished the Transitions study, they had the option to either stay in my group, joining the Transformation Group, or getting into a women's ministry groups.

We hosted pot-luck birthday celebrations every two months. Then on special occasions—including Easter—we celebrated birthdays and Easter! Rita, a Transformations leader, became the party planner. Everyone would help, but she was the one that would put her heart into all our celebrations and always made them special.

There were others who supported our group in many different ways. God was planting His seeds of hope in all of us as we were growing in faith together.

Prison Ministry

In addition to the Tuesday night Transitions class, I was asked to teach Saturday classes forty miles away, at the women's prison in Jean. Cheri, one of the women in my Transitions group, drove with me to assist with the class. She was also a part of the Las Vegas Prison Ministry. We enjoyed long talks about our purpose, and we prayed for and encouraged one another to keep Christ first place in our life.

We started classes in the secure lock-up facility. Each Tuesday, a guard was required to escort us to the class location. Once, as a guard escorted me to the building where the class was being held, he asked me why I was coming here and mentoring women who were in prison. I looked at him and said "The reason I come here is because the Lord is here." He looked at me like I was crazy, but I hope it gave him something to think about. Where the broken are, there the Lord is.

A couple of days before Christmas, Cheri called and asked if I would go with her to the Las Vegas prison on Christmas Eve. The prison rules stated that too few women with security clearance in the visiting room during visiting hours meant that some of the women would not be able to see their children.

They were having a hard time finding people to volunteer on Christmas Eve. We were there a couple of hours and as we were getting ready to leave an intellectually handicapped young girl came over, gave me a hug, and thanked me for being there so she could see her mommy! What a blessing for the little girl, the mom, and me to experience God's love. My time at the prison was fruitful. The women needed encouragement and hope that could only come from Christ.

After a year and a half, it was getting more and more difficult for me to make the trip, so I had to give up the ministry.

Transitions became God's Gift to Many. Watching Christ heal so many broken women was a blessing for me. Christ was helping all of us heal from our past hurts. I realized that Christ put the compassion and love for these women in my heart, so I could serve Him by serving them.

"'For I know the plans I have for you,' declares the Lord, 'plans to prosper you and not to harm you, plans to give you hope and a future. Then you will call on me and I will listen to you. You will seek me and find me when you seek me with all your heart'" (Jeremiah 29:11-13).

CHAPTER EIGHT

TRANSITIONS' IMPACT: TESTIMONIES OF PARTICIPANTS

Gabriela

I was young and naive. I married a person that was abusive in every way, but I didn't see it until the abuse got quite frequent and intense. With the help of a counselor, I moved out after two years of marriage. I had enough courage to move out, not enough to divorce him, after all   God hates divorce. I felt stuck; I couldn't move forward, and I didn't want to move backwards I read about Transitions in the church bulletin, and I enrolled immediately. It seemed perfect for me.

Transitions helped me to understand the dynamics of the abusive relationship, the destructive dance that my ex-husband and I had been dancing, the hole in which I kept falling into, and the lies that I kept believing for years. But most importantly, Transitions gave me the tools to stop the cycle and start writing a different story for my life. I started building self-esteem, self-confidence, and a strong relationship with God. I also learned about boundaries and assertiveness. The group leader was nothing but an inspiration, and my peers became my accountability partners in time of weakness. Together, we went through the tough times and came out the other side healed, restored, loved, and affirmed.

Transitions is a much needed support group. Most abuse happens behind closed doors and there aren't that many places where the victim can go. Transitions is a safe place where women could get help and clarity, wisdom and understanding, love and healing.

God hates divorce, but he allows it in certain circumstances to protect the victim. And God is a God of second chances. He gave me a fresh start. With the new tools that I got from Transitions, I was able to build a healthy relationship, and God blessed me with a loving husband and two beautiful babies.

My past is behind, the wounds healed, the lesson learned, and my present keeps blossoming before my very own eyes. I know that it is God who orchestrates everything for the good of those who love him. God planted a seed in Joyce's heart; that seed became Transitions, and it has touched and transformed so many lives already. I am one of them, and I will forever be grateful.

Author's Comments: Gabriela was my Co-Leader when I first started Transitions. She was bright and enthusiastic. Her inspiration and support was one of God's gifts to our support group.

Nancy

Transitions has been the start of the transformation of my healing. Ever since I walked through the doors, it has been a life changing experience, from January 2009 to the present.

I was very apprehensive at first and had a hard time opening up, even though I knew in my heart and soul that I was in the right place. That night Joyce handed me a guide line on various topics that would be discussed. After being in the group for few weeks, I knew this was the support group I was looking for. Self-esteem, boundaries, toxic people, emotions, and depression were a few of the many topics in the coming weeks.

Transitions has been a life-changing experience. This support group helped me resolve issues from my past and heal some old wounds. Weeks turned into months, and months turned into years and slowly God transformed me into a stronger woman which gave me the desire and ambition to help others. Transitions brought me out of my darkness into the light, so I could feel safe and secure again. Doors are now always opening and I am a new me. I've witnessed radical changes and spiritual growth. Where I was once ordinary; I am now "extraordinary".

Today, my motto is to live your faith by example. That was the key that unlocked my success. God has brought me full circle. I know he has been at the center of our support group and inside these remarkable women's hearts.

Transitions women that stay the course are like caterpillars. We started out crawling and afraid, but as we learned and grew, God gave us the courage to become butterflies, with freedom to spread our wings and fly.

Authors Comments: Nancy was very helpful by sending emails reminding women of special events and schedule changes. She has a heart of gold and was always very supportive and encouraging. She has moved to New York; we still keep in touch by email and phone calls.

Rita

I was very self-sufficient and was ignoring and refusing invitations to mingle with any group in the church. For me, there are other ways to acquire God's wisdom and to apply and share them, including sharing the other blessings/gifts that he bestowed upon me. I realized to practice what I preached, I needed to be plugged into a Christian group and not just attend Sunday services. I curiously chose Transitions from the list of groups without even having a clue that it would become a take-off for me of a flight on a different path.

My wings now are flying in the fields of facilitating and leading a class, coordinating and co-leading events, which I never liked to do before, except for my family. But what counts the most is the continuous flow of Jesus's love, wisdom, power and the "in dwelling" of the Holy Spirit in me and my sisters in Christ. I realize God's blessings on our group because we were receiving God's love and mercy through the in-dwelling of the Holy Spirit.

Author's Comments: Rita was like a little flower that blossomed. At first, she was hesitant to join and then she not only joined in, we nominated her to coordinate of all the celebrations, and she became one of the Transformation group leaders. She has since moved to the orient. I miss her optimistic attitude and her friendship. She is and always will be a loyal friend. She keeps me updated on what she is doing through Facebook. Rita is an example of Transitions being God's gift to many. She has started a group in the Orient.

Candy

You have such a desire to do God's work and to help the women through their hurts to know God; I can feel your passion.

Even as we stumble through life in our attempts to do the right things, if we follow God's plan and directions, He will guide us.

It is through the trust we have in Him that we can be bold and step out in Love and Faith.

You have shown us how to do that and have encouraged us to do the same, God must be truly proud of you, and He has blessed us all.

Thank you for showing us the Love of God and His plan for us.

Your Friend in Christ, Candy

Author's Comments: Candy has a big heart and amazing insight to spiritual issues. She helped keep the group strong and focused. I loved her hugs and her sense of humor. We still keep in touch.

Sunshine

In July 2009, I knew I had had enough. My life was not going how I wanted it to go, and I had finally realized that I might have something to do with it. I needed to make some changes right away. I decided to reach out to the church Central Christian that I had gone to a few times over the last five years while being in Las Vegas. While looking on their website, I found the Thursday night class called Transitions and thought to myself, that is what I am going through right now, a "transition." Luckily, that next day was a Thursday, and I took the long walk from the parking lot into the church, down to the classroom, where the class was being held. Joyce Lewis came up to me, hugged me, and introduced herself. I sat down and waited to see what this was all about. Joyce told her story which was similar to mine. Then as the other ladies began to share a little about themselves, I found that we all had a tremendous amount in common. That night we talked about self-esteem, which God knew I needed to hear.

I have always struggled with my view of myself and finding the positive attributes that I have. Every Thursday, I would show up for the meeting and leave with another tool in my toolbox to help myself begin to heal, with God right by my side. As the weeks passed, I began to notice changes in my attitude and outlook on my life. I began to realize more and more that if I stuck to God's plan for me instead of always trying to do life my way, life could be a lot easier, and maybe even happy. The bonds and friendships that were cultivated, will always be in my memories and a part of my heart. I have become a more open, spiritual, faithful, peaceful, strong woman, and it is because God nudged (actually shoved) me to Transitions and Joyce Lewis.

It is now a year later, July 17, 2010, and I am well on my walk with Jesus Christ. I have been able to pass on some of the tools I have gained to my three beautiful daughters, whom I want to have the highest regard for themselves as humanly possible. All it took was for me to surrender and God has made the rest possible.

Glory be to GOD Sunshine

Author's Comments: Sunshine was an inspiration to the group. She had a fun personality—always willing to help. My prayer for her is that she uses her skills. It was such a pleasure to have her as part of our group and watch her grow.

Deena

In 2009, after a marriage of 21 years that entailed episodic abuse, I finally divorced my ex-husband. After the divorce, I lived like a "prodigal" daughter full of sin. However, there was a hunger within my heart, so I continued to search. God led me to Central Christian church. I attended church once in a while, because it was far from my residence. When I had heard about the Divorce Care Class at Central, I decided to check it out. It was free of charge, and I thought I could learn more about divorce and how to heal from it.

That first night, was surreal to me. I participated first in worship then everyone was instructed to break out and go to the meeting room of their selected group. I must have looked lost because a female pastor approached me and asked "What class or group are you seeking to attend?" and I replied, "I was looking for the Divorce Care group." She responded, "Just follow this group of ladies." So I followed the group of ladies and discovered after everyone took their seats that it was a support group for women called "Transitions." God knows best and knew what I truly needed in order to inspire my rebirth in Jesus Christ and return to God's path. God knew I needed not only a "safe" place to ignite my passion for him, but to learn and grow closer to him, in order to heal, love, and trust again.

God provided me this resource, Transitions, a support group and stepping stone to being reborn and renewed in Christ. That first night at Transitions stirred my soul and triggered my mind to spin like a whirl. In fact, my mind raced all the way home during the thirty-minute drive. As I got ready for bed, my mind was still racing on past experiences and the newly found lesson of the types of forgiveness that enriched me. I knew of asking God and others for forgiveness, but forgiveness for myself struck like a jolt of lightening within me. It felt like a brand new feeling to me. God graciously and mercifully wanted me to truly know, feel, and live his ultimate love for me by forgiving me and giving up his one and only Son for my sins. At that moment, I learned and felt secure in God's love and I could finally forgive myself.

Upon awaking the next morning I felt cleansed, so exu-berant, and filled with peace! It was that morning I chose to surrender my life to Christ and live God's way. This significant choice and continuing to live daily for Christ has granted me an abundant life. God's gracious blessings has garnered me angels, sincere friends, and family along with health, and even obtaining the unimaginable, a doctorate in education. In addition, he afforded me a Life Coach Certification in Integrative Health and Wellness. My hopes are to serve him and a second chance at building a sacred marriage with a man whose heart is for God as he designed.

If you are in a position where you feel lost and uncertain, seek God and partake of all he offers. Evidently, all God's works, promises and resources, like Transitions can ignite your faith. God provided for me at the most appropriate time the essential tools for spiritual growth, personal development, healing, and endless love to uncover my true purpose; to be his righteous daughter, a servant, obediently serving him, like Jesus and encouraging others to uncover and discover God's desire and will for their lives.

Author's comments: Deena was such a support to all the women in Transitions. She was so generous with her time and gifts. She also was a big help with all our group activities. We still keep in touch and support each other in our faith walk. She is truly a sister in Christ.

She is very dedicated to her faith; her friends and family are very proud of her many achievements. She graduated with honors and is continually being ask to speak on her doctorate dissertation.

Personal Notes

Thank you for showing me how the power of our Lord and savior works in women who are united in faith.

I wanted to tell you just how much your classes have helped me and to say thank you for letting Jesus Christ work through you. Your classes have taught me that I am loved and not alone. You have taught me that I deserve to be treated with respect and do not have to put up with abuse. Thank you for your faith in God and for teaching us that through our relationship with Christ we can heal.

The first step to fixing something is recognizing there is a need for repair. The loss of self was evident in each individual. We turned ourselves over to the Lord and surrendered. What I will remember most about Transitions is that we are no longer alone, and we are here to start a new beginning. Transitions amplifies what true love is all about; loving someone for who they are.

My life has changed since I've met you. You've helped me become more secure and to find my worth through God. I've learned to stand up for myself. Thanks so much.

You'll never know the difference you've made. Love you so much, One of your Transitions student. Thank you for showing me how the power of our Lord our savior works in women who are united in faith.

The Shadows of His hand - by Judith Couchman

During times of brokenness we realize that our ways, our plans and desires, aren't working. When we hand our lives back to God, He pours His desires into our hearts to accomplish His work, His way.

Joyce,

Your passion and God's calling in your life is so evident.

*Thanks for your faithfulness for allowing God to
use you from your place of brokenness.*

*In Christ,
Marj Counselor at Central*

Article published in *Central Beat Magazine*

*Overcoming dysfunction. Joyce Lewis is passionate about helping
women deal with past hurts from abusive relationships. Realizing
from her own experience how tough it was to live in dysfunction,
Joyce began volunteering her time at a battered women's shelters.
Led by God, Joyce began leading a Support Group at Central, called
Transitions. She wrote the scripture-based curriculum herself based
on her own family relationships, research and encounters with other
abused women. Joyce's desire is to help with the transitional process
of moving women forward with their lives. She helps women from
all walks of life talk about their emotions, fear, resentment, anger
and even grief. When asked what women take from this class, Joyce
says, "Hope and a light at the end of the tunnel." We all looked
forward to our Thursday nights together. We supported each other,
as we were learning and growing on our faith journey, together.*

CHAPTER NINE

FAITH IS A JOURNEY, NOT A DESTINATION

I knew my mom would need full-time care soon. We had Hospice come and evaluate her condition. Due to her heart condition, she qualified for help. Bob and I knew mom couldn't live with us in our tri-level condo, so we decided to purchase a new house.

Across the highway was a new home development. I fell in love with one of the models, so we found a lot and broke ground. The house was big enough for my mom to have her own room and bathroom, and we still had a guest room for visitors. Her bedroom was on one side of the house and ours was on the other. Hospice was there three times a week to help with her personal needs. God's timing is always perfect. We were just getting settled in our new home, when I received an email from Michael Hamilton, a Christian newspaper reporter from Auckland, New Zealand. We met Michael at a Crystal Cathedral Christmas Celebration. Michael was a supporter of the Hour of Power.

He was very interested in my support group and wanted Bob and me to come to New Zealand to participate in the New Zealand's Forum on the Family. The forum gathers all different organizations and church's together to address family issue. The event included guest speakers who addressed children's issues including abuse, drugs and alcohol, and media influence.

The forum represented more than eighty groups and was being held in Auckland. Some of the organizations present included: Focus on the Family, Family Life International, Voice for Life, National Council of Women. Michael wanted a representative from Central, myself, and Bob to come out for two-and-one-half weeks to attend the conference. He was willing to arrange for us to go on the radio, set up meetings with different churches and organizations, and talk to them about my program. Pastor Steven Cuss wrote a letter of introduction for us.

To Whom It May Concern,

Emotional Abuse is a silent, sometimes invisible and dangerous plague affecting every neighborhood in every city in the world. While survivors of emotional abuse easily categorized, many find themselves stuck feeling hopeless and either exhausted or fearful of reaching out for help.

Thankfully, help reaches out to them—in a community called Transitions.

Transitions is a safe, welcoming, spiritual community transitioning emotionally abused survivors from victim to leader facilitated by an emotionally abused survivor.

It is 2 Corinthians 1: 3,4 in action. "Praise be to the God and Father of our Lord Jesus Christ, the Father of compassion and the God of all comfort, who comforts us in all our troubles, so that we can comfort those in any trouble with the comfort we ourselves have received from God."

The true genius of Transitions is its model of healing and growth for women who are or have been in abusive relationships. Through Transitions they learn their value as a Christ follower. They discover how Christ can use them and their testimony to serve other women in their predicament.

Joyce Lewis founded Transitions over 9 years ago and has seen the program go full cycle as her "alumni" have moved from victim to leader in their community. Joyce is herself a survivor of abusive relationships. She is a living, breathing illustration of 2 Corinthians 1. I have witnessed firsthand her heart and character and how God uses Joyce and her Transitions program to reach women who think they are unreachable. I offer my highest recommendation of Joyce as a person and her Transitions program. I believe God is opening doors wide open for Joyce to develop Transitions in communities all around the world.

Kind Regards, Steve Cuss Lead Pastor
Discovery Christian Church

We did attend the forum and met with many organizations involved in counseling, support of families and marriages, violence and abuse area, and various social issues. The problems we have in the area of violence and abuse is all over the world. No one seemed to have answers to the problems the world is facing. My belief is and always will be is that God is the way to the truth, light, and the love that this world so desperately needs. Christ gives us love through the Holy Spirit. From His love we get strength that helps us heal from our brokenness.

We checked into the Auckland Hilton, our home for the next five days. While there, we celebrated our twenty-second wedding anniversary.

Our Wedding Anniversary Celebration

Pastor Steve's letter was very helpful as we were meeting with various, counselors and organizations. Most of the people we met with were interested in my program. They invited me back and said if I could come back for a few months they would be glad to work with me. Someday I may go back to New Zealand and be able to help them start a program. Only God knows!

We rented a car and headed south; our destination was Christ Church. Michael had arranged for us to stay at one of the pastor's homes there. After a few stops along the way, we found our way to Pastor Daphne and her husband David's house. We remained with them for two nights, and they helped us with our tour arrangements. Their house was in the hills surrounded by trees. There were a lot of stairs to get inside the home, and a porch wrapped around the whole house. Daphne and David were very good to us. We learned a lot about their culture while we visited. They attended a humanitarian church, Spreydon Baptist Church. Their mission was to help abused women and the disabled. They were truly doing the Lord's work. We went to their church and was a part of their Bible study and prayer meditation group. What a humbling experience. Daphne and David had so much love for the Lord and for each other.

They had pet chickens that made their home on the porch. Every morning, David would go out to feed them and they would follow him around the porch waiting for him to give them breakfast. He was like a mother hen with her chicks. What a blessing it was to stay in their home and share our faith.

When it was time to go home, we headed for the Christ Church airport. We missed home, but we were not looking forward to the long flight.

We picked up my mother and returned to our new house. We were all thankful to be home.

My mom was very supportive of the Transitions group. I hosted celebrations at our house, so mom got to know the women. Mom looked forward to their visits. The church made a prayer quilt for my mom, and all the women in Transitions made a circle and we asked for God's blessing for my mother. My mother and I became closer during the time she was with us. (She and I were not close during my growing up years.) I would read scripture to her and talk with her about how wonderful it was going to be in heaven with Christ. She used to kiss my hand and tell me I was her angel. When we could no longer physically take care of her, we had to move her to a Hospice recommended home.

My mom passed away in September, 2012, at age ninety-nine. When she died, I felt at peace. Bob and I watched over her for twelve years.

In December, 2012, I decided to stop teaching Transitions. After eleven years, I needed spiritual renewal. Some of the women in Transformation and I discussed the possibility of us offering both Transitions and Transformation seminars at different churches. We were then meeting at the Renewing Life Center.

Some of the women had issues that I wasn't aware of. After our discussion of the problems that they brought up, I decided that doing the seminars was my idea and not God's.

Christ was always opening doors for me, and now he was closing a door. My ministry was my world for so many years. God put me in this valley to restore me and to move me forward. I went through depression for two weeks. I felt like I had let Jesus and the women in my group down. God had other plans for me.

The Renewing Life Center goal is that every person who walks through their door experience excellent care and affordable care. The center has three purposes. The first purpose is to provide excellent and compassionate Christian counseling. The second is to give care for pastors, ministry leaders, and their families. The third purpose is to provide spiritual formation and direction to help people grow in their relationship with God.

The center was offering a Transforming Lives Program. This study was a twenty-four week discipleship study for transforming the soul, heart, mind, and body.

The study gave me the opportunity to evaluate where I was in my faith walk and to heal from the valley that I was in. Christ was in this valley with me, helping me heal through the Holy Spirit. I was a strong support group leader and Christ wanted me to become a humble student, so I could become a humble child of God.

The classes on taking hold of the real presence of God's healing of our wounds, sins, and defenses by His loving grace, were so helpful in my effort to break free from the past to see the present.

Bob and I decided that we needed to attend a church closer to home. One of my P.E.O sisters was going to Faith Christian Church in Boulder City, so we decided to attend. After several visits we decided to become members. Pastor Brent Williams is a great minister with a good message.

Faith Christian Church

We're a life-giving church.
We're a come as you are church.
We're a Bible believing church.
We're a loving family.
We're a place where people can find a second chance.
We're a mission minded church with a servant attitude.
We're a church that has vibrant, heart-felt worship.

We reach out because people matter to God.

We were very blessed to find Faith Christian Church. Shortly after we joined, we experienced major challenges. I had been having trouble with my knees, and my doctor said my left knee needed to be replaced and I needed three shots (one week apart) on my right one. Shortly after that news, my daughter told me that she had breast cancer. She had to go through chemotherapy, radiation, and then a double mastectomy. Our family got together in California to discuss how we could help her during this horrific time in her life.

The blessing in this testing is that it brought our family closer together by loving Terri during this difficult time in her life. The first thing I did was postpone my surgery so I could take care of her after her chemotherapy sessions. Her dad lived in California and was able to go to her doctor appointments with her. Her children lived nearby and would be a big help. After her surgery, Bob and I spent eight days with her while she was recovering from her surgery. She is cancer free but still has a lot of health issues to overcome; she is always in our prayers.

The next blessing in the testing is that my grandchildren had children. My grandson had a daughter that he adores and my granddaughter had a son that is the love of her life. My daughter gets so much pleasure being with her grandchildren. This has tremendously helped her take her mind off of all her health issues.

My knee surgery was in July, and my doctor recommended a recovery facility for three weeks. I had my own private room; the staff and physical therapist were excellent. I felt Christ was watching over me, I called my room my God cave. I thanked the Lord every day for my loving friends, P.E.O. sisters, and neighbors. Pastor Brent came twice to visit and pray with me. Three of the women from the Transitions group came to visit and brought a Joyce Meyer video. They were all there to help, I felt so blessed.

I was glad to see 2015 end and 2016 begin. As I reflected back, I thought of the blessings and the lessons I learned through the testing's. By staying in faith, all the things I went through made me a stronger Christian. "When I said, "My foot is slipping," your unfailing love, Lord, supported me. When anxiety was great within me, your consolation brought me joy" (Psalm 94:18,19).

A portion of our family lives near Garden Grove, California. When we are there, we attend Shepherd's Grove Church. Bobby Schuller is the lead pastor (Robert H. Schuller's grandson). He has written books including *Imagine Happiness: A Simple Guide*, and the trilogy, *Know the Love of God Forever, Love Your Soul as God Loves You,* and *Show the Love of God to Others.* We met Bobby in Israel on the Crystal Cathedrals "One Light One World" tour. Crystal Cathedral's Founder Pastor Robert H. Schuller started the *Hour of Power*, televising his positive message around the world. Bobby has continued the *Hour of Power* program at Shepherd's Grove. We are so pleased that he started his own church and was able to continue. He is truly a man of God and has a servant's heart!

I'm not what I do.
I'm not what I have.
I'm not what people say about me.
I am the beloved of God.
It's who I am.
No one can take it from me.
I don't have to worry.
I don't have to hurry.
I can trust my friend Jesus
and share His love
with the world.
--Pastor Bobby Schuller

CHAPTER TEN

FINISHING WELL

Writing this book gave me time to reflect on my successes, accomplishments, weaknesses, and failures. There are things I would change, and there are things I feel blessed to have had the opportunity to experience.

I have had to climb out of many trials and valleys during my lifetime. When I gave Christ my heart and accepted Him as my Lord and Savior, He recreated me from a self-centered dysfunctional woman to a God-centered humble woman. My problems became challenges. "I can do all things through Him who gives me strength" (Philippians 4:13). Christ is the light in my life; I trust Him to always be the light that leads me out of the valleys of darkness. "God has not given me a spirit of fear, but of power, love and of a sound mind" (2 Timothy 1:7). As I went through the painful experiences in my life, He has proven His faithfulness over and over again. Faith has given me the courage to face my enemies. The purpose that He has given me—to help abused women—has blessed my life in many ways. I pray to Christ every day that the Holy Spirit will continue to give me the wisdom to make Godly decisions for the rest of my life.

Part of God's healing process was for me to search my heart and ask myself if I had truly forgiven all the people

69

that caused me pain. This was a challenge for me and I had some soul searching to do before I could actually say that I have unconditional love for the people who have hurt me. I realized that if I did not forgive everybody in my life, even my enemies, that I would not be forgiven.

Pastor Charles Stanley once said, "Forgiveness is never complete until first, we have experienced the forgiveness of God, second, we can forgive others who have wronged us, and third, we are able to forgive ourselves."

Forgiveness was a process for me. I didn't want to go through all of the emotional hurts that I had gone through all over again. The Lord opened my eyes to His unconditional love, which strengthened me. I realized that forgiveness obliterates bitterness, envy, hatred, and regret. Understanding that all these feelings were only hurting me, the Lord was able to release all these feelings through the Holy Spirit. I was able to forgive and was set free.

Bob and I have always tried to be there for our family. It hasn't been easy keeping up with five children, seven grandchildren, seven spouses, and seven great-grand-children. We both have tried to bring love and joy to their lives. We love them all, and they are always in our prayers. We give thanks to the Lord for our blended family and cherish the memories we created through the years.

Bob and I have been looking back on our life together and we realized that our faith has brought us to a place where we are better equipped to go through the challenges of the aging process. Bob has some short-term memory loss, which has been a challenge for both of us. We both first met the news with denial, anger, fear, and all the other emotions people feel when they grieve. After praying about my reactions, the Holy Spirit asked me a question: "Who Are You in Christ?" When I realized my reaction was out of fear instead of love, my whole attitude changed. Bob and I were able to talk about our feelings and have an optimistic outlook for the future. We are staying strong and walking with the Lord one day at a time. We are still a team, and we work out our problems together. The Lord blessed us with each other. Because of the medication and our love for each other,

Bob is doing much better. Throughout the years of study and experiencing Christ's love, grace, and mercy, I discovered that loving well has everything to do with finishing well. As I was growing in faith, God always opened doors of opportunity as soon as He knew I was ready to take my faith journey to the next level.

A friend of mine told me about a class that was being offered at a church in Boulder City. The class is based on the book *Emotionally Healthy Spirituality* by Peter Scazzero. This study helped me understand that it is impossible to be spiritually mature, while remaining emotionally immature.

Through this class, which has given me insights into my spiritual strengths and weaknesses, I have learned that we need to go through many obstacles to grow and learn God's ways. But to me, His way is the only way. As I shared this information with my husband both of us realized how important God's guidance and wisdom is to get us through this life-changing journey together. As we prayed and continued to turn to God for answers, He has not let us down. Through His love for us, we are able to continue our love story even in the hardest of times. God has given us His gift of patience, kindness, and understanding. But the most important gift that He has given us is the unconditional love that we have for each other.

Life without faith is not an option for me. Faith, to me, means God the Creator owns my heart and my soul, He has set me free, so I can continue to fulfill my purpose, to continue *Planting Seeds of Hope*. My plan for the future is to spread the good news of the Gospel by sharing my story. Also, to encourage churches to start support groups. Everyone has a story, and as Christians we need to support each other in every stage of our faith walk. There are many challenges for women who have experienced emotional abuse. If the Lord opens more doors of opportunity, I would like to have seminars on the subject of abuse and dysfunctional families.

"Come to me, all you who are weary and burdened, and I will give you rest. Take my yoke upon you and learn from me, for I am gentle and humble in heart, and you will find rest for your souls" (Matthew 11: 28-29).

Through my faith journey, I have tried to stay strong and to take the advice of a poem that Mother Teresa had on her wall for children in Calcutta (author unknown):

People are often unreasonable, irrational, and self-centered.
Forgive them anyway.

If you are kind, people may accuse you of selfish, ulterior motives.
Be kind anyway.

If you are successful, you will win some unfaithful
friends and some genuine enemies.
Succeed anyway.

If you are honest and sincere people may deceive you.
Be honest and sincere anyway.

What you spend years creating, others could destroy overnight.
Create anyway.

If you find serenity and happiness, some may be jealous.
Be happy anyway.

Give the best you have, and it will never be enough.
Give your best anyway.

In the final analysis, it is between you and God.
It was never between you and them anyway.

My goal is that at the end of my life, I would not have a single bit of talent left, so I can say, "I tried to use everything Christ gave me, for His glory".

Writing the final chapter was almost like writing the last chapter of my life. Only God knows what my last chapter will be. I am excited about the new doors of opportunity He will open for me to share my story and testimony.

ABOUT THE AUTHOR

Her husband and she are still living in Boulder City, Nevada. She is still a member of P.E.O. and on the Board of Directors at the Boulder City Senior Center. Both Joyce and her husband are still members of Faith Christian Church, which has become their church family.